The Animal Alphabet

A is for ant-eater with its long snout,
B is for bats which zigzag about,
C for the chimp who swings from a branch,
D for the donkey asleep after lunch,
E is for elephant, wrinkly and grey,
F for the fox which I hope gets away,
G for giraffe with its JCB neck,
H is the hen with a husband to peck,
I for an indolent iguana,
J for the shape of the monkey's banana,
K for koala who clings to a tree,
L for the leopard whose spots won't change me,
M is for mole, my namesake, of course,
N for the neigh of a bad-tempered horse,
O is the ostrich whose head disappears
And (wait for it, wait for it, cover your ears)
P for the parrot which squawks till you're deaf,
Q is for quails' eggs, a treat from the chef,
R for rhinoceros, beware its huge horn,
S for the sloth who's too lazy to yawn,
T is the tiger, that striped mega-star,
U is for ugly which no creatures are,
V is for vole, so nearly my name
(Just change the first letter and read it again),
W watch out for Ahab's white whale,
X for the slobbery kiss of a snail,
Y for the Yogi in Yellowstone Park,
Zzzz for the forest asleep after dark.

John Mole

OXFORD
UNIVERSITY PRESS

Great Clarendon Street, Oxford OX2 6DP

Oxford University Press is a department of the University of Oxford.
It furthers the University's objective of excellence in research, scholarship,
and education by publishing worldwide in

Oxford   New York

Auckland   Cape Town   Dar es Salaam   Hong Kong   Karachi
Kuala Lumpur   Madrid   Melbourne   Mexico City   Nairobi
New Delhi   Shanghai   Taipei   Toronto

With offices in

Argentina   Austria   Brazil   Chile   Czech Republic   France   Greece
Guatemala   Hungary   Italy   Japan   Poland   Portugal   Singapore
South Korea   Switzerland   Thailand   Turkey   Ukraine   Vietnam

Oxford is a registered trade mark of Oxford University Press
in the UK and in certain other countries

First published 2001
First published in paperback 2005

British Library Cataloguing in Publication Data

Data available

ISBN: 978-0-19-276326-6

3 5 7 9 10 8 6 4

Typeset by Mary Tudge (Typsetting Services)

Printed in China by Printplus

My First Oxford Book of Animal Poems

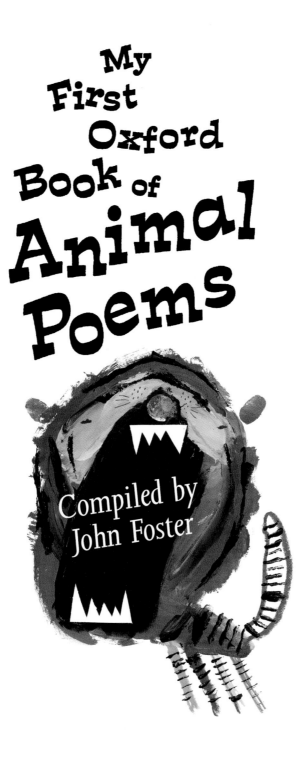

Compiled by
John Foster

OXFORD
UNIVERSITY PRESS

Contents

The Animal Alphabet   John Mole   1

Around the House and in the Garden

In Nooks and Crannies and Under the Ground

Across the Fields and in the Woods

In the Zoo and at the Wildlife Park

In the Forest and Far Away

Beside the Sea, Beneath the Waves

Around the House

Chanticleer

High and proud on the barnyard fence
Walks rooster in the morning.
He shakes his comb, he shakes his tail,
And gives his daily warning.

'Get up, you lazy boys and girls,
It's time you should be dressing!'
I wonder if he keeps a clock,
Or if he's only guessing.

Anon.

and in the Garden

The Dobermann Dog, O the Dobermann Dog

The Dobermann dog, O the Dobermann dog,
O why did they buy me the Dobermann dog?
He is bigger than I am
by more than a half
and so clumsy at play
it would make a cat laugh—
he sprawls and he falls
over tables and chairs
and goes over his nose when he
stalks down the stairs.
He's the colour of seedcake
mixed with old tar
and he never knows rightly
where his feet are—
he growls in a fashion
to bully all Britain
but it doesn't so much as
frighten my kitten.
On the table at tea-time
he rests his big jaw
and rolls his gentle eyes
for one crumb more.
How often he tumbles me
on the green lawn
then he licks me and stands
looking rather forlorn
like a cockadoo waiting the
sun in the morn.
I call him my Dobe
O my Dobermann dog
my Obermann Dobermann
yes, my Octobermann
Obermann Dobermann dog.

George Barker

My Puppy

It's funny
my puppy
knows just how I feel.

When I'm happy
he's yappy
and squirms like an eel.

When I'm grumpy
he's slumpy
and stays at my heel.

It's funny my puppy
knows such a great deal.

Aileen Fisher

Goldfish

One small fish in a
Polythene bag;
Can't swim round, can
Only look sad.
Take a pair of scissors,
Snip a quick hole,
Down flops water
And fish into a bowl!

She waits a little moment,
Flips her tail free,
Then off into circles
As frisky as can be.
Dash-about—splash-about—
Do what you wish:
You're mine, you black-spotted
Cheeky-eyed
Fish!

John Walsh

The Gerbil

The gerbil stands up
Crouching like a kangaroo
Ready to hop;
To him the children he sees
Seem tall as trees;
His paws clutch
The teacher's hand
That stretches like a branch
Above the sand
Of the tiny desert
In his hutch.

Stanley Cook

Our Hamster's Life

Our hamster's life:
there's not much
to it,
not much
to it.

He presses his pink nose
to the door of his cage
and decides for the fifty-six
millionth time
that he can't get
through it.

Our hamster's life:
there's not much
to it,
not much
to it.

It's about the most boring
life in the world,
if he only
knew it.
He sleeps and he drinks and he eats.
He eats and he drinks and he sleeps.

He slinks and he dreeps.
He eats.

This process
he repeats.

Our hamster's life:
there's not much
to it,
not much
to it.

You'd think it would drive him bonkers,
going round and round on his wheel.
It's certainly driving me bonkers,

watching him
do it.
But he may be thinking:
'That boy's life,
there's not much
to it,
not much
to it:

watching a hamster go round on a wheel.
It's driving me bonkers if he only knew it,

watching him
watching me
do it.'

Kit Wright

The Song of the Mischievous Dog

There are many who say that a dog has its day,
  And a cat has a number of lives;
There are others who think that a lobster is pink,
  And that bees never work in their hives.
There are fewer, of course, who insist that a horse
  Has a horn and two humps on its head,
And a fellow who jests that a mare can build nests
  Is as rare as a donkey that's red.
Yet in spite of all this, I have moments of bliss,
  For I cherish a passion for bones,
And though doubtful of biscuit, I'm willing to risk it,
  And I love to chase rabbits and stones.
But my greatest delight is to take a good bite
  At a calf that is plump and delicious;
And if I indulge in a bite at a bulge,
  Let's hope you won't think me too vicious.

Dylan Thomas

Cats

Cats sleep
Anywhere,
Any table,
Any chair,
Top of piano,
Window-ledge
In the middle,
On the edge,
Open drawer,
Empty shoe,
Anybody's
Lap will do,
Fitted in a
Cardboard box,
In the cupboard
With your frocks—
Anywhere!
They don't care!
Cats sleep
Anywhere.

Eleanor Farjeon

To a Squirrel at Kyle-na-no

Come play with me;
Why should you run
Through the shaking tree
As though I'd a gun
To strike you dead?
When all I would do
Is to scratch your head
And let you go.

W. B. Yeats

Squirrel

Oh the elephant strolls, the turkey struts,
But the squirrel leaps from tree to tree.
He is lithe and swift, he is nuts on nuts
But he will not wait for me.

The blindworm slithers, the monkey swings,
But the squirrel flies like a bird.
When I begged him to teach me how
He pretended he hadn't heard.

Oh the panther pounces, the cheetah pads,
The lynx slinks, (the skunk stinks) and rabbits run.
But I wanted to leap like a squirrel
And before I could ask him he was gone.

James Fenton

Sparrow

A hummingbird hums.
A woodpecker drums.
A gull is graceful in flight.
A jay finds fighting
Pretty exciting
And licks every bird in sight.
A swallow swoops
In up-and-down loops
And seldom lights on the ground.
But take a sparrow
Whose world is narrow,
A sparrow just hangs around.

A partridge whirrs
Through the pines and firs.
A chickadee's ways are cute.
A pigeon coos
And an owl hoo-hoos
Whenever it gives a hoot.
A crow steals corn
From the year it's born
Then hides where it can't be found.
A sparrow, though,
Doesn't come and go
A sparrow just hangs around.

Kaye Starbird

Little Bird

Little hurt bird
in my hand
your heart beats
like the pound of the sea
under the warmth
of your soft feathers.

Charlotte Zolotow

The Corn Scratch Kwa Kwa Hen and the Fox

And the Corn Scratch Kwa Kwa Hen
Heard the grumbling rumbling belly
Of the Slink Back Brush Tail Fox
A whole field away.

And she said to her sisters in the henhouse,
'Sisters, that Slink Back Brush Tail Fox
Will come and here's what we must do,'
And she whispered in their sharp sharp ears, 'kwa, kwa.'

And when that Slink Back Brush Tail Fox
Came over the field at night,
She heard his paw slide on a leaf,
And the Corn Scratch Kwa Kwa Hen and her sisters
Opened their beaks and—

'KWA!'
The moon jumped
And the Chooky Chook Chicks
Hid under the straw and giggled,
It was the LOUDEST KWA in the world.

And the Log Dog and the Scat Cat
And the Brat Rat and the House Mouse
And the Don't Harm Her Farmer
And his Life Wife and their Shorter Daughter
And their One Son came running,

On their slip slop, flip flop,
Scatter, clatter, slick flick, tickly feet
And they opened their mouths and shouted—

'FOX!'
And it was the LOUDEST NAME in the world.
And the Slink Back Brush Tail Fox
Ran over the fields and far away
And hid in a hole with his grumbling rumbling belly.

And the Corn Scratch Kwa Kwa Hen
Tucked the Chooky Chook Chicks under her feathers
And said, 'kwa,'
And it was the softest kwa in the world.

Julie Holder

19

Robin

Where have the birds gone
one by one?
Off to the south
and after the sun.

Only the robin,
with breast of red,
hops in the garden
and cocks his head,

fluffs up his feathers
and flits to the sill,
pecking up crumbs
as the air grows chill.

Tony Mitton

Old Shellover

'Come!' said Old Shellover.
'What?' says Creep.
'The horny old Gardener's fast asleep;
The fat cock Thrush
To his nest has gone;
And the dew shines bright
In the rising Moon;
Old Sallie Worm from her hole doth peep:
'Come!' said Old Shellover.
'Ay!' said Creep.

Walter de la Mare

Cat in the Dark

Mother, Mother, what was that?
Hush, my darling! Only the cat.
(Fighty-bitey, ever-so-mighty)
Out in the moony dark.

Mother, Mother, what was that?
Hush, my darling! Only the cat.
(Prowly-yowly, sleepy-creepy,
Fighty-bitey, ever-so-mighty)
Out in the moony dark.

Mother, Mother, what was that?
Hush, my darling! Only the cat.
(Sneeky-peeky, cosy-dozy,
Prowly-yowly, sleepy-creepy,
Fighty-bitey, ever-so-mighty)
Out in the moony dark.

Mother, Mother, what was that?
Hush, my darling! Only the cat.
(Patchy-scratchy, furry-purry,
Sneeky-peeky, cosy-dozy,
Prowly-yowly, sleepy-creepy,
Fighty-bitey, ever-so-mighty)
Out in the moony dark.

Margaret Mahy

The Fallow Deer at the Lonely House

One without looks in tonight
    Through the curtain-chink
From the sheet of glistening white;
One without looks in tonight
    As we sit and think
    By the fender-brink.

We do not discern those eyes
    Watching in the snow;
Lit by lamps of rosy dyes
We do not discern those eyes
    Wondering, aglow,
    Four-footed, tiptoe.

Thomas Hardy

In Nooks and Crannies

Four Things

There be four things which are little upon the earth,
but they are exceeding wise.

The ants are a people not strong,
yet they prepare their meat in the summer;

The conies are but a feeble folk,
yet they make their houses in the rocks;

The locusts have no king,
yet they go forth all of them by bands.

The spider taketh hold with her hands
and is in kings' palaces.

The Bible, Proverbs 30

and Under the Ground

Caterpillar

Once a chubby caterpillar
Sat upon a leaf,
Singing, 'Eat, eat and be merry—
Life is very brief.'

Soon he lost his appetite
And changed his merry tune.
He started spinning, hid himself
Inside a hard cocoon.

And he was still and quiet there—
Day after day went by.
At last it cracked and he emerged,
A gorgeous butterfly.

He spread his brown and crimson wings
And warmed them in the sun
And sang, 'Now I must see the world—
My life has just begun.'

Wendy Cope

Spin Me a Web, Spider

Spin me a web, spider,
Across the window-pane
For I shall never break it
And make you start again.

Cast your net of silver
As soon as it is spun,
And hang it with the morning dew
That glitters in the sun.

It's strung with pearls and diamonds,
The finest ever seen,
Fit for any royal king
Or any royal queen.

Would you, could you, bring it down
In the dust to lie?
Any day of the week, my dear,
Said the nimble fly.

Charles Causley

Tell Me, Little Woodworm

Tell me, little woodworm
Eating through the wood
Surely all that sawdust
Can't do you any good.

Heavens! Little woodworm
You've eaten all the chairs
So that's why poor old Grandad's
Sitting outside on the stairs.

Spike Milligan

Mice

I think mice
Are rather nice.

      Their tails are long,
      Their faces small,
      They haven't any
      Chins at all.
      Their ears are pink,
      Their teeth are white,
      They run about
      The house at night.
      They nibble things
      They shouldn't touch
      And no one seems
      To like them much.

But I think mice
Are nice.

Rose Fyleman

I Knew a Black Beetle

I knew a black beetle, who lived down a drain,
And friendly he was, though his manners were plain;
When I took a bath he would come up the pipe
And together we'd wash and together we'd wipe.

Though mother would sometimes protest with a sneer
That my choice of a tub-mate was wanton and queer,
A nicer companion I never have seen;
He bathed every night, so he must have been clean.

Whenever he heard the tap splash in the tub
He'd dash up the drain-pipe and wait for a scrub,
And often, so fond of ablution was he,
I'd find him there floating and waiting for me.

But nurse has done something that seems a great shame:
She saw him there, waiting, prepared for a game:
She turned on the hot and she scalded him sore
And he'll never come bathing with me any more.

Christopher Morley

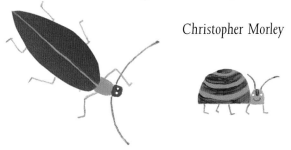

The Centipedes in My Garden

The centipedes in my garden
  Are such noisy little brutes,
I wish that they'd wear slippers
  Instead of hobnail boots.

Martin Honeysett

Only My Opinion

Is a caterpillar ticklish?
  Well, it's always my belief
That he giggles, as he wriggles
  Across a hairy leaf.

Monica Shannon

Ants, Although Admirable, Are Awfully Aggravating

The busy ant works hard all day
And never stops to rest or play.
He carries things ten times his size,
And never grumbles, whines, or cries.
And even climbing flower stalks,
He always runs, he never walks.
He loves his work, he never tires,
And never puffs, pants, or perspires.

Yet though I praise his boundless vim
I am not really fond of him.

Walter R. Brooks

The Fly

How large unto the tiny fly
Must little things appear!—
A rosebud like a featherbed,
Its prickle like a spear;

A dew-drop like a looking glass,
A hair like golden wire;
The smallest grain of mustard-seed
As fierce as coals of fire;

A loaf of bread, a lofty hill,
A wasp, a cruel leopard;
And specks of salt as bright to see
As lambkins to a shepherd.

Walter de la Mare

The Mole

The mole for breakfast likes to munch
A dozen worms: the same for lunch.
For tea and supper—can you guess?
More worms, you say? The answer's yes.
And after dark, so it is said,
The mole keeps worms beside its bed.
In fact the humble mole can do
What is impossible for you.
(Unless you are prepared to say
You could eat sixty worms a day?)

Dick King-Smith

Lizard

A flash of green,
a flicker of light,
a gleam of gold
    glittering
just out of sight.

A heat-hazed wall,
a wreath of vine,
a glint of eye
    blinking
in bright sunshine.

A zap of speed,
a glimmer of jade,
a hint of movement
    diving
deep into shade.

Moira Andrew

Hurt No Living Thing

Hurt no living thing:
    Ladybird, nor butterfly,
Nor moth with dusty wing,
    Nor cricket chirping cheerily,
Nor grasshopper, so light of leap,
    Nor dancing gnat, nor beetle fat,
Nor harmless worms that creep.

Christina Rossetti

Ladybird! Ladybird!

Ladybird! Ladybird! Fly away home,
Night is approaching, and sunset is come:
The herons are flown to their trees by the Hall;
Felt, but unseen, the damp dewdrops fall.
This is the close of a still summer day;
Ladybird! Ladybird! Haste! Fly away!

Emily Brontë

Across the Fields

At Sunrise

Across the silent paddock
There comes a cautious hare,
His ears, two pointed fingers,
To probe the frosty air.
And where the wheat is growing
He pauses in his run
Along the aisles of morning,
To breakfast with the sun.

Max Fatchen

and in the Woods

A New-Born Foal

kicked itself to life
still sleepy

struggled
on jelly legs
to get up

sniffed around
with its trembling nose

nuzzled its mum
for a mouthful of milk

then tottered off
long and lanky
to say hello to the world.

Patricia Leighton

Spring

Now the sleeping creatures waken—
  Waken, waken;
Blossoms with soft winds are shaken—
  Shaken, shaken;
Squirrels scamper and the hare
Runs races which the children share
Till their shouting fills the air.

Now the woodland birds are singing—
  Singing, singing;
Over field and orchard winging—
  Winging, winging;
Swift and swallow unaware
Weave such beauty on the air
That the children hush and stare.

Raymond Wilson

The Polliwog

Oh, the Polliwog is woggling
  In his pleasant native bog
With his beady eyes a-goggling
  Through the underwater fog
And his busy tail a-joggling
  And his eager head agog—
Just a happy little frogling
  Who is bound to be a Frog!

Arthur Guiterman

The Donkey

When fishes flew and forests walked
   And figs grew upon thorn,
Some moment when the moon was blood
   Then surely I was born;

With monstrous head and sickening cry
   And ears like errant wings,
The devil's walking parody
   On all four-footed things.

The tattered outlaw of the earth,
   Of ancient crooked will;
Starve, scourge, deride me: I am dumb,
   I keep my secret still.

Fools! For I also had my hour;
   One far fierce hour and sweet:
There was a shout about my ears,
   And palms before my feet.

G. K. Chesterton

Mare

When the mare shows you
her yellow teeth, stuck
with clover and gnawed leaf,
you know you have combed
pastures of spiky grasses,
and tough thickets.

But when you offer her
a sweet, white lump
from the trembling plate
of your palm—she trots
to the gate, sniffs—
and takes it with velvet lips.

Judith Thurman

The Cow

The friendly cow all red and white,
    I love with all my heart;
She gives me cream with all her might,
    To eat with apple tart.

She wanders lowing here and there,
    And yet she cannot stray,
All in the pleasant open air,
    The pleasant light of day;

And blown by all the winds that pass
    And wet with all the showers,
She walks among the meadow grass
    And eats the meadow flowers.

Robert Louis Stevenson

Rabbit and Lark

'Under the ground
    It's rumbly and dark
And interesting,'
    Said Rabbit to Lark.

Said Lark to Rabbit,
    'Up in the sky
There's plenty of room
    And it's airy and high.'

'Under the ground
    It's warm and dry.
Won't you live with me?'
    Was Rabbit's reply.

'The air's so sunny.
    I wish you'd agree,'
Said the little Lark,
    'To live with me.'

But under the ground
    And up in the sky,
Larks can't burrow
    Nor rabbits fly.

So Skylark over
    And Rabbit under
They had to settle
    To live asunder.

And often these two friends
    Meet with a will
For a chat together
    On top of the hill.

James Reeves

Tortoise and Hare Poem
(or: Slow, slow, quick, quick slow . . .)

Slowly the tortoise raised her head,
stared slowly at the hare;
slowly stepped towards the line
and waited there.

Calmly she heard the starting gun,
crawled calmly down the track;
calmly watched the hare race on
with arching back.

Quickly the hare ran out of sight,
chased quickly through the wood;
quickly fled through fern and moss,
through leaf and mud.

Swiftly he leapt past hedge and field,
sped swiftly for his prize;
briefly stopped to take a rest—
and closed his eyes.

Slowly the tortoise reached the wood,
slowly she ambled on.
The hare raced proudly through his dreams;
the tortoise won.

Judith Nicholls

The Duck

Behold the duck.
It does not cluck.
A cluck it lacks.
It quacks.
It is especially fond
Of a puddle or pond.
When it dines or sups
It bottoms up.

Ogden Nash

Blue Herons

One swoops in on a glider wing
Two stick-picks the shore

Three stands stiff as a soldier boy
Waiting for soldier four

Five parades in his downy coat
Six inspects a toad

Seven leans into a singing wind
Eight's on the river road

Nine flies up to the bird-bent tree
Ten wears a midnight plume

Eleven talks back to the gossipy wren
Twelve's in his watery room

J. Patrick Lewis

Little Trotty Wagtail

Little trotty wagtail, he went in the rain,
And tittering, tottering sideways he ne'er got straight again,
He stooped to get a worm, and looked up to catch a fly,
And then he flew away ere his feathers they were dry.

Little trotty wagtail, he waddled in the mud,
And left his little footmarks, trample where he would.
He waddled in the water-pudge and waggle went his tail,
And chirrupt up his wings to dry upon the garden rail.

Little trotty wagtail, you nimble all about,
And in the dimpling water-pudge you waddle in and out;
Your home is nigh at hand and in the warm pigsty,
So, little Master Wagtail, I'll bid you a goodbye.

John Clare

Minnows

Swarms of minnows show their little heads,
Staying their wavy bodies 'gainst the streams,
To taste the luxury of sunny beams
Tempered with coolness. How they ever wrestle
With their own sweet delight, and ever nestle
Their silver bellies on the pebbly sand.
If you but scantily hold out the hand,
That very instant not one will remain;
But turn your eye, and they are there again.

John Keats

The Bird's Nest

I know a place, in the ivy on a tree,
Where a bird's nest is, and the eggs are three,
And the bird is brown, and the eggs are blue,
And the twigs are old, but the moss is new,
And I go quite near, though I think I should have heard
The sound of me watching, if I had been a bird.

John Drinkwater

The Woodpecker

The woodpecker pecked out a little round hole,
And made him a home in the telephone pole.

One day when I watched he poked out his head,
And he had on a hood and a collar of red.

When the streams of rain pour out of the sky,
And the sparkles of lightning go flashing by,

And the big, big wheels of thunder roll,
He can snuggle back in the telephone pole.

Elizabeth Madox Roberts

The Owl Looked Out of the Ivy Bush

The owl looked out of the ivy bush
And he solemnly said, said he,
'If you want to live an owlish life
Be sure you are not like me.

'When the sun goes down and the moon comes up
And the sky turns navy blue,
I'm certain to go tu-whoo tu-whit
Instead of tu-whit tu-whoo.

'And even then nine times out of ten
(And it's absolutely true)
I somehow go out of my owlish mind
With a whit-tu whoo-tu too.'

'There's nothing in water,' said the owl,
'In air or on the ground
With a kindly word for the sort of bird
That sings the wrong way round.'

'I might,' wept the owl in the ivy bush,
'Be just as well buried and dead.
You can bet your boots no one gives two hoots!'
'Do I, friend my,' I said.

Charles Causley

The Owl

When cats run home and light is come
  And dew is cold upon the ground,
And the far off stream is dumb,
  And the whirring sail goes round,
  And the whirring sail goes round—
    Alone and warming his five wits,
    The white owl in the belfry sits.

When merry milkmaids click the latch,
  And rarely smells the new mown hay,
And the cock hath sung beneath the thatch
  Twice or thrice his roundelay,
  Twice or thrice his roundelay—
    Alone and warming his five wits,
    The white owl in the belfry sits.

Alfred, Lord Tennyson

Swans in the Night

Three swans
Under the moon,
Three shadows
On the lagoon.

Three swans
On the water ride,
Three shadows
Move beside.

Silver water,
Silent swans,
Swaying ferns
With silvered fronds.

A strolling cloud
Obscures the moon,
Gone the swans
From the dark lagoon.

Joan Mellings

Goodnight

'Goodnight,' said the frog,
'I am burrowing deep
Into the mud for my winter sleep.'

'Goodnight,' said the hedgehog,
'I'm off to my nest,
It's time I went for a good long rest.'

'Goodnight,' said the bat,
'My feet are strong
I'll hang in a cave the winter long.'

'Goodnight,' said the dormouse,
'I shall be
Curled in my nest at the foot of the tree.'

'Goodnight,' said the toad,
'I've found a deep hole
To keep me warm from the winter's cold.'

'When you wake in the spring,'
Said the kindly sun,
'I'll be here with my warmth for everyone.'

June Crebbin

In the Zoo and at

Our Visit to the Zoo

When we went to the Zoo
We saw a gnu,
    An elk and a whelk
And a wild emu.

We saw a hare
And a bear in his lair,
    And a seal have a meal
On a high-backed chair.

We saw a snake that was
    Hardly awake,
And a lion eat a meal
They'd forgotten to bake.

We saw a coon and a baby baboon,
The giraffe made us laugh
All afternoon!

We saw a crab
And a long-tailed dab
    And we all went home
In a taxi-cab.

Jessie Pope

the Wildlife Park

Meeting the Snake

I used to fear you,
slithery snake,
the way you move,
the shapes you make.

But now I've met you
at the zoo,
I've changed the way
I think of you.

I used to think you
slippy, sly.
And yet I find you
clean and dry,

and soft and slow
and good to touch.
So now I do not fear you,
much.

Tony Mitton

Gorilla

Gorilla thinks
We're tiny,
Gorilla thinks
We're bare,
Gorilla thinks
That eating greens
Might help us
Grow more hair!
Gorilla thinks
We're nosy,
Gorilla thinks
We stare,
Gorilla thinks
We'd make good pets . . .
And he wants
THAT one THERE!

Sue Cowling

Tiger

I'm a tiger
Striped with fur
Don't come near
Or I might Grrr
Don't come near
Or I might growl
Don't come near
Or I might
BITE!

Mary Ann Hoberman

Polar Bear

Hugging the wall, down
there in his open pit
he ambles absently,
fitting his whole body
to the wide curve
of dingy cement.

Backwards and forwards
loping, big head weaving
pressing one matted flank
and then the other
to the sun-scorched cliff
of his lonely prison.

His coat is far from white—rather
a drab cream, with
yellow or brownish stains.
—He looks unhappy in the heat.
No wonder he never

turns to growl at
us, begging for attention.

James Kirkup

I'm a Parrot

I am a parrot
I live in a cage
I'm nearly always
in a vex-up rage

I used to fly
all light and free
in the luscious green
forest canopy

I am a parrot
I live in a cage
I'm nearly always
in a vex-up rage

I miss the wind
against my wing
I miss the nut
and the fruit picking

I am a parrot
I live in a cage
I am nearly always
in a vex-up rage

I squawk I talk
I curse I swear
I repeat the things
I shouldn't hear

So don't come near me
or put out your hand
because I'll pick you
if I can
pickyou
pickyou
if I can

I want to be Free
Can't You Understand

Grace Nichols

A Robin Redbreast in a Cage

A robin redbreast in a cage
Puts all Heaven in a rage.
A dove-house filled with doves and pigeons
Shudders Hell thro' all its regions.
A dog starved at the master's gate
Predicts the ruin of the State.
A horse misused upon the road
Calls to Heaven for human blood.
Each outcry of the hunted hare
A fibre from the brain does tear.
A skylark wounded in the wing,
A cherubim does cease to sing.

William Blake

Sea Lions

The satin sea lions
Nudge each other
Toward the edge
Of the pool until
They fall like
Soft boulders
Into the water,
Sink down, slide
In swift circles,
Twist together
And apart, rise again
Snorting, climb
Up slapping
Their flippers on
The wet cement:
Someone said
That in all the zoo
Only the sea lions
Seem happy.

Valerie Worth

Giraffes

Giraffes
   I like them
   Ask me why
      Because they hold their heads up high.
      Because their necks stretch to the sky.
      Because they're quiet and calm and shy.
      Because they run so fast they fly.
      Because their eyes are velvet brown.
      Because their coats are spotted tan.
      Because they eat the tops of trees.
      Because their legs have knobbly knees.
      Because
      Because. That's why
I like giraffes.

Mary Ann Hoberman

Circus Elephant

Does the Elephant remember
In the grey light before dawn,
Old noises of the jungle
In mornings long gone?

Does the Elephant remember
The cry of hungry beasts;
The Tiger and the Leopard,
The Lion at his feasts?

Do his mighty eardrums listen
For the thunder of the feet
Of the Buffalo and Zebra
In the dark and dreadful heat?

Does His Majesty remember,
Does he stir himself and dream
Of the long-forgotten music
Of a long-forgotten stream?

Kathryn Worth

When You Talk to a Monkey

When you talk to a monkey
    He seems very wise.
He scratches his head
    And he blinks both his eyes;
But he won't say a word.
    He just swings on a rail
And makes a big question mark
    Out of his tail.

Rowena Bennett

The Peacock

The peacock,
somewhat overdressed
for an ordinary day,
comes rainbow shimmering
across the ordered lawns.

His sweeping tail
brushes the close-cropped grass,
as, with the merest bow,
he accepts the adoration
of the gaping crowd.

With regal pomp
he gloriously unfurls
the iridescent splendour
of his jewelled tail
and, emperor-like, stands proud.

But then, he goes too far;
he tries to sing.
An eerie, plaintive wail rings out.
A noise not fitting in the least,
for such a sumptuous king.

Cynthia Rider

Noah's Arks

They must hurry aboard
   Before it's too late;
As their homes disappear
   There's no time to wait.
For the fields and the forests,
   The rivers and trees
Are shrinking and sinking
   Beneath human seas.

So in cages, enclosures,
   Reservations and parks,
They're taken aboard
   The animal arks.
And just like Noah,
   They wait inside
     To disembark
When the seas subside.

Pat Moon

In the Forest

The Little Hiawatha

Then the little Hiawatha
Learned of every bird its language,
Learned their names and all their secrets;
How they built their nests in Summer,
Where they hid themselves in Winter,
Talked with them whene'er he met them,
Called them 'Hiawatha's Chickens'.

Of all beasts he learned the language,
Learned their names and all their secrets,
How the beavers built their lodges,
How the squirrels hid their acorns,
How the reindeer ran so swiftly,
Why the rabbit was so timid:
Talked with them whene'er he met them,
Called them 'Hiawatha's Brothers'.

Henry Wadsworth Longfellow

and Far Away

Bees, Bothered by Bold Bears, Behave Badly

'Your honey or your life!' says the bold burglar bear,
As he climbs up the tree where the bees have their lair.
  'Burglars! Burglars!' The tree begins to hum.
    'Sharpen up your stings, brothers! Tighten up your
      wings, brothers!
Beat the alarm on the big brass drum!
  Watch yourself, bear, for
    here
      we
        come!'

Then the big black bees buzz out from their lair,
With sharp stings ready zoom down on the bear.
  'Ouch! Ouch! Ouch! Don't be so rough!'
    He slithers down the tree, squalling. 'Hey, let me
      be!' Bawling,
  'Keep your old honey. Horrid sticky stuff!
    I'm going home, for
      I've
        had
          enough!'

Walter R. Brooks

Wolf

Mine is the howl
that chills the spine
in the forest gloom;
mine is the whine.

Mine is the nose
that breathes in fear
when danger's close;
mine is the ear.

Mine is the fur
the huntsmen trade;
mine is the fur,
I am afraid.

Judith Nicholls

The World Is Full of Elephants

The world is full of elephants,
the baby ones and taller ones.
African elephants have great big ears,
the Indian ones have smaller ones.

Gavin Ewart

Don't Call Alligator Long-Mouth Till You Cross River

Call alligator long-mouth
call alligator saw-mouth
call alligator pushy-mouth
call alligator scissors-mouth
call alligator raggedy-mouth
call alligator bumpy-bum
call alligator all dem rude word
but better wait
      till you cross river.

John *Agard*

Hippopotamuses

Hippopotamuses never
Put on boots in rainy weather.
To slosh in mud up to their ears
Brings them great joy and merry tears.
Their pleasure lies in being messed up
They just won't play at being dressed up.
In fact a swamp is heaven plus
If you're a hippopotamus.

Arnold *Spilka*

Zebra

Who let them loose
    with face paints?
Who gave them pyjamas
    to wear?
Who made them look
    like newspapers?
Who striped them
    here and there?

Who designed them
    like mint humbugs?
Who painted them
    white and black?
Who thought of
    a different pattern
For each new-born
    zebra's back?

Moira Andrew

The Lion

The lion just adores to eat
A lot of red and tender meat,
And if you ask the lion what
Is much the tenderest of the lot,
He will not say a roast of lamb
Or curried beef or devilled ham

Or crispy pork or corned-beef hash
Or sausages or mutton-mash.
Then could it be a big plump hen?
He answers 'No'. What is it then?
Oh, lion dear, could I not make
You happy with a lovely steak?

Could I entice you from your lair
With rabbit pie or roasted hare?
The lion smiled and shook his head.
He came up very close and said,
'The meat I am about to chew
Is neither steak nor chops. It's you.'

Roald Dahl

Won't!

Shan't!

Don't!

Can't!

Commissariat Camels

We haven't a camelty tune of our own
To help us trollop along,
But every neck is a hair-trombone
(*Rttt-ta-ta-ta!* is a hair-trombone!)
And this is our marching-song:
Can't! Don't! Shan't! Won't!
Pass it along the line!
Somebody's pack has slid from his back,
Wish it were only mine!
Somebody's load has tipped off in the road—
Cheer for a halt and a row!
Urr! Yarrh! Grr! Arrh!
Somebody's catching it now!

Rudyard Kipling

The Yak

As a friend to the children commend me the Yak.
    You will find it exactly the thing:
It will carry and fetch, you can ride on its back,
    Or lead it about with a string.

The Tartar who lives on the plains of Tibet
    (A desolate region of snow)
Has for centuries made it a nursery pet,
    And surely the Tartar should know!

Then tell your papa where the Yak can be got,
    And if he is awfully rich
He will buy you the creature—or else he will not.
    (I cannot be positive which.)

Hilaire Belloc

Poor Design

Said a certain young adder on shedding his skin:
'It's much worse getting out than it was getting in.
These coats would be very much simpler to strip
If they'd only remember to put in a zip!'

Jiri Havel

Snake

The boa constrictor's a slippery snake
Who slithers and slides round his tree,
And when tasty animals wander too close
He squashes them slowly for tea.

Giles Andreae

A Dream of Elephants

I dreamed a dream of elephants.
I cannot tell you why.
But in my dream I saw the herd
go slowly walking by.

They moved beneath a blazing sun,
through rising dust and heat.
They made their solemn journey
on strong and silent feet.

And as I watched, the steady herd
walked slowly, sadly by,
until I stood, amazed, alone,
beneath a silent sky.

I watched them as they moved away.
I watched as they walked on.
They merged into the heat and dust
till all of them were gone.

I dreamed a dream of elephants.
I cannot tell you why.
But in my dream I saw the herd
go slowly walking by.

Tony Mitton

Late one night in Kalamazoo

Late one night in Kalamazoo,
the baboons had a barbecue
the kudus flew a green balloon,
the poodles yodelled to the moon.

A monkey strummed a blue guitar;
a donkey caught a falling star,
a camel danced with a kangaroo,
late one night in Kalamazoo.

Jack Prelutsky

Grandpa Bear's Lullaby

The night is long
But fur is deep,
You will be warm
In winter sleep.

The food is gone
But dreams are sweet
And they will be
Your winter meat.

The cave is dark
But dreams are bright
And they will serve
As winter light.

Sleep, my little cubs, sleep.

Jane Yolen

Beside the Sea,

Whale

Wouldn't you like to be a whale
And sail serenely by—
An eighty-foot whale from your tip to your tail
And a tiny, briny eye?
Wouldn't you like to wallow
Where nobody says 'Come out!'?
Wouldn't you love to swallow
And blow all the brine about?
Wouldn't you like to be always clean
But never have to wash, I mean,
And wouldn't you love to spout—
    O yes, just think—
A feather of spray as you sail away,
And rise and sink and rise and sink,
And blow all the brine about?

Geoffrey Dearmer

Beneath the Waves

The Lobster Quadrille

'Will you walk a little faster?' said a whiting to a snail,
'There's a porpoise close behind us, and he's treading on my tail.
See how eagerly the lobsters and the turtles all advance!
They are waiting on the shingle—will you come and join the dance?
    Will you, won't you, will you, won't you, will you join the dance?
    Will you, won't you, will you, won't you, won't you join the dance?

'You can really have no notion how delightful it will be
When they take us up and throw us, with the lobsters, out to sea!'
But the snail replied 'Too far, too far!' and gave a look askance—
Said he thanked the whiting kindly, but he would not join the dance.
    Would not, could not, would not, could not, would not join the dance.
    Would not, could not, would not, could not, could not join the dance.

'What matters it how far we go?' his scaly friend replied.
'There is another shore, you know, upon the other side.
The further off from England, the nearer is to France—
Then turn not pale, beloved snail, but come and join the dance.
    Will you, won't you, will you, won't you, will you join the dance?
    Will you, won't you, will you, won't you, won't you join the dance?'

Lewis Carroll

Seal

See how he dives
From the rocks with a zoom!
See how he darts
Through his watery room
Past crabs and eels
And green seaweed,
Past fluffs of sandy
Minnow feed!
See how he swims
With a swerve and a twist,
A flip of the flipper,
A flick of the wrist!
Quicksilver-quick,
Softer than spray,
Down he plunges
And sweeps away:
Before you can think,
Before you can utter
Words like 'Dill pickle'
Or 'Apple Butter',
Back up he swims
Past sting ray and shark,
Out with a zoom,
A whoop, a bark;
Before you can say
Whatever you wish,
He plops at your side
With a mouthful of fish!

William Jay Smith

Three Little Puffins

Three little puffins
　　Were partial to muffins,
As partial as partial can be,
　　They wouldn't eat nuffin
　　But hot buttered muffin
For breakfast and dinner and tea.

　　Pantin' and puffin'
　　And chewin' and chuffin'
They just went on stuffin', dear me!
　　Till the three little puffins
　　Were chockful of muffins
And puffy as puffy can be.
　　　　　　　　　　All three
　　Were puffy as puffy can be.

Eleanor Farjeon

The Lugworm and the Haddock

Said the lugworm from its burrow
To the haddock in the sea,
'How'd you like a worm for dinner?
Well, you won't catch little me,'
And it laughed and wriggled round
Safely hidden underground.

Said the haddock to the lugworm
'It's a miracle to me
How you make those cunning burrows
In the sand beneath the sea.
I could never dig one, never,
But you lugworms, you're so clever!'

Said the lugworm, swelling proudly,
'If you're good, I'll let you see
How we start to dig our tunnels
So deep down and cleverly.
Wait one moment up I come.'
'Gulp,' the haddock said. 'Yum, yum.'

Richard Edwards

Penguins on Ice

Every penguin's mum
can toboggan on her tum.
She can only do that
as she's fluffy and fat:

It must be nice
to live on ice.

Every penguin's dad
is happy and glad.
He can slip and slide
and swim and glide:

It must be nice
to live on ice.

All penguin chicks
do slippery tricks.
They waddle and fall
but don't mind at all:

It must be nice
to live on ice.

Celia Warren

My Other Granny

My granny is an Octopus
    At the bottom of the sea,
And when she comes to supper
    She brings her family.

She chooses a wild wet windy night
    When the world rolls blind
As a boulder in the night-sea surf
    And her family troops behind.

The sea-smell enters with them
    As they slide and slither and spill
With their huge eyes and their tiny eyes
    And a dripping ocean-chill.

Some of her cousins are lobsters
    Some floppy jelly-fish—
What would you be if your family tree
    Grew out of such a dish?

Her brothers are crabs jointed and knobbed
    With little pinhead eyes,
Their pincers crack the biscuits
    And they bubble joyful cries.

Crayfish the size of ponies
    Creak as they sip their milk.
My father stares in horror
    At my mother's secret ilk.

They wave long whiplash antennae,
    They sizzle and they squirt—
We smile and waggle our fingers back
    Or Grandma would be hurt.

'What's new, Ma?' my father asks,
    'Down in the marvellous deep?'
Her face swells up, her eyes bulge huge
    And she begins to weep.

She knots her sucker tentacles
    And gapes like a nestling bird,
And her eyes flash, changing stations,
    As she attempts a WORD.

Then out of her eyes there brim two drops
    That plop into her saucer—
And that is all she manages,
    And my dad knows he can't force her.

And when they've gone, my ocean-folk,
    No man could prove they came—
For the sea-tears in her saucer
    And a man's tears are the same.

Ted Hughes

The Fish With the Deep Sea Smile

They fished and they fished
Way down in the sea,
Down in the sea a mile.
They fished among all the fish in the sea,
For the fish with the deep sea smile.

One fish came up from the deep of the sea
From down in the sea a mile,
It had blue-green eyes
And whiskers three
But never a deep sea smile.

One fish came from the deep of the sea,
From down in the sea a mile.
With electric lights up and down his tail,
But never a deep sea smile.

They fished and they fished
Way down in the sea,
Down in the sea a mile.
They fished among all the fish in the sea,
For the fish with the deep sea smile.

One fish came up with terrible teeth,
One fish with long strong jaws,
One fish came up with long stalked eyes,
One fish with terrible claws.

They fished all through the ocean deep,
For many and many a mile.
And they caught a fish with a laughing eye,
But none with a deep sea smile.

And then one day they got a pull,
From down in the sea a mile.
And when they pulled the fish into the boat,
HE SMILED A DEEP SEA SMILE.

And as he smiled, the hook got free,
And then, what a deep sea smile!
He flipped his tail and swam away,
Down in the sea a mile.

Margaret Wise Brown

86

Sea Gull

The sea gull curves his wings,
the sea gull turns his eyes.
Get down into the water, fish!
(if you are wise.)

The sea gull slants his wings,
the sea gull turns his head.
Get deep into the water, fish!
(or you'll be dead.)

Elizabeth Coatsworth

Dolphin Dance

We are darters and divers
from secret sea-caves.
We're divers and gliders,
we dance through the waves.

We spiral and curl,
we weave as we fly,
stitch shimmering arches
from ocean to sky.

Judith Nicholls

A Baby Sardine

A baby Sardine
Saw her first submarine:
She was scared and watched through a peephole.

'Oh, come, come, come,'
Said the Sardine's mum,
'It's only a tin full of people.'

Spike Milligan

Sea Horse

O under the ocean waves
I gallop the seaweed lanes,
I jump the coral reef,
And all with no saddles or reins.

I haven't a flowing mane,
I've only this horsy face,
But under the ocean waves
I'm king of the steeplechase.

Blake Morrison

The Crab that Writes

When the tide is low on moonlit nights,
Out of the sea crawls the crab that writes,
Out of the sea crawls the crab whose claw
Writes these words on the shining shore:

> *Pebble mussel*
> *Fin and scale*
> *Sole and mackerel*
> *Skate and whale*
> *Seaweed starfish*
> *Salt and stone*
> *Sand and shell and cuttlebone.*

When the tide is low on moonlit nights,
Back to the sea crawls the crab that writes,
Back to the sea crawls the crab whose claw
Leaves these words on the shining shore:

> *Pebble mussel*
> *Fin and scale*
> *Sole and mackerel*
> *Skate and whale*
> *Seaweed starfish*
> *Salt and stone*
> *Sand and shell and cuttlebone.*

Richard Edwards

The Walrus

The widdly, waddly walrus
has flippery, floppery feet.
He dives in the ocean for dinner
and stands on his noggin to eat.

The wrinkly, crinkly walrus
swims with a debonair splash.
His elegant tusks are of ivory
and he wears a fine walrus moustache.

The thundery, blundery walrus
has a rubbery, blubbery hide.
He puffs up his neck when it's bedtime
and floats fast asleep on the tide.

Jack Prelutsky

Seal Lullaby

Oh! Hush thee, my baby,
The night is behind us,
And black are the waters
That sparkled so green.
The moon, o'er the combers,
Looks downward to find us
At rest in the hollows
That rustle between.

Where billow meets billow,
Then soft be thy pillow,
Ah, weary wee flipperling,
Curl at thy ease.
The storm shall not wake thee,
Nor shark overtake thee,
Asleep in the arms
Of the slow-swinging seas.

Rudyard Kipling

Index of First Lines and Titles

First lines are in italics

Index of Authors & Illustrators

David Broadbent
pp. 14–15, 42–3, 62–3.

Lindsey Gardiner
pp. 10–11, 12–13, 54–5, 61,
70–1, 84–5.

Ben Challenor
pp. 3, 16–17, 34–5,
48–9, 56–7.

Alan Marks
pp. 1, 22–3, 32–3, 38, 41,
50–1, 64, 68–9, 76–7,
80–1, 90–1, 96.

Mary McQuillan
pp. 26–7, 44–5, 72–3,
82–3, 88–9.

Mark Marshall
pp. 8–9, 18–19, 24–5,
36–7, 52–3, 66–7,
78–9.

Emma Rivett
pp. 20–1, 28–9, 30–1,
46–7, 58–9, 74–5,
86–7.

Acknowledgements

John Agard: 'Don't Call Alligator Long-Mouth Till You Cross River' from *Say it Again, Granny* (Bodley Head, 1986), repr. by permission of The Random House Group Ltd. **Giles Andreae:** 'Snake' from *Rumble in the Jungle* (Orchard Books, 1996), repr. by permission of Orchard Books, a division of The Watts Publishing Group Ltd, 96 Leonard Street, London, EC2A 4XD. **Moira Andrew:** 'Lizard' and 'Zebra', both copyright © Moira Andrew 1998 from *The Wider World* ed. Robyn Gordon (Riverpoint Publishing, 1998), repr. by permission of the author. **George Barker:** 'The Doberman Dog, O the Doberman Dog' from *Runes and Rhymes and Tunes and Chimes* (Faber & Faber, 1969), repr. by permission of the publisher. **Hillaire Belloc:** 'The Yak' from *Cautionary Verses* (Duckworth, 1970), copyright © The Estate of Hillaire Belloc 1970, repr. by permission of PFD on behalf of The Estate of Hillaire Belloc. **Rowena Bennett:** 'When You Talk to a Monkey' from *Singing in the Sun* ed. Jill Bennett (Viking Kestrel, 1988). **Walter R. Brooks:** 'Ants, Although Admirable, Are Awfully Aggravating' and 'Bees, Bothered By Bold Bears, Behave Badly' both from *The Collected Poems of Freddy The Pig* (Overlook Press), repr. by permission of the publisher. **Charles Causley:** 'Spin Me a Web, Spider' from *Early in the Morning* (Penguin, 1988) and 'The Owl Looked Out of the Ivy Bush' from *Collected Poems for Children* (Picador, 1996), both repr. by permission of David Higham Associates Ltd. **G. K. Chesterton:** 'The Donkey' from *Collected Poems* (1927), repr. by permission of A. P. Watt Ltd on behalf of The Royal Literary Fund. **John Clare:** 'Little Trotty Wagtail' copyright © Eric Robinson 1984, repr. by permission of Curtis Brown Group Ltd, London on behalf of Eric Robinson. **Stanley Cook:** 'Gerbil' from *The Squirrel in Town* (Blackie, 1988), repr. by permission of Sarah Matthews. **Wendy Cope:** 'Caterpillar', copyright © Wendy Cope 2001, first pub. in this collection by permission of the author. **Sue Cowling:** 'Gorilla', copyright © Sue Cowling 2001, first pub. in this collection by permission of the author. **June Crebbin:** 'Goodnight' from *Cows Moo Cars Toot* (Viking, 1995), copyright © June Crebbin 1995, repr. by permission of Penguin Books Ltd. **Roald Dahl:** 'The Lion' from *Dirty Beasts* (Jonathan Cape, 1983), repr. by permission of Random House Group Ltd and David Higham Associates. **Walter de la Mare:** 'Old Shellover' and 'The Fly' both from *The Complete Poems of Walter de la Mare* (Faber & Faber, 1969), repr. by permission of the Literary Trustees of Walter de la Mare and the Society of Authors as their representative. **Geoffrey Dearmer:** 'Whale' from *Round the World Poetry*, repr. by permission of Juliet Woollcombe. **John Drinkwater:** 'The Bird's Nest' from *Eric Carle's Animals Animals* (Hodder & Stoughton, 1990), repr. by permission of Samuel French Ltd, on behalf of the Estate of John Drinkwater. **Richard Edwards:** 'The Lugworm and the Haddock' from *Teaching the Parrot* (Faber & Faber, 1996) and 'The Crab that Writes' from *Moon Frog* (Walker Books, 1993), both repr. by permission of the author. **Gavin Ewart:** 'The World is Full of Elephants' from *Caterpillar Stew* (Hutchinson, 1990), repr. by permission of Mrs M. A. Ewart. **Eleanor Farjeon:** 'Cats' from *Blackbird Has Spoken* (Macmillan, 1999) and 'Three Little Puffins' from *The Silver Curlew* (Samuel French/OUP), both repr. by permission of David Higham Associates Ltd. **Max Fatchen:** 'At Sunrise' from *A Paddock of Poems* (Angus & Robertson, 1980), repr. by permission of John Johnson (Authors' Agents) Ltd. **James Fenton:** 'Squirrel', copyright © James Fenton, from *Allsorts 5* (Macmillan), repr. by permission of PFD on behalf of James Fenton. **Aileen Fisher:** 'My Puppy' from *Up the Windy Hill*, copyright © Aileen Fisher 1953, 1981, repr. by permission of Marian Reiner Literary Agent. **Rose Fyleman:** 'Mice' from *Fifty-One New Nursery Rhymes* copyright © 1931, 1932 by Doubleday, a division of Bantam Doubleday Dell Publishing Group Inc., repr. by permission of Doubleday, a division of Random House Inc., and The Society of Authors as the Literary Representatives of the Estate of Rose Fyleman. **Jiri Havel:** 'Poor Design' from *Animals Have Lots of Fun*, trans. by Stephen Finn (Treasure Press, 1986). **Mary Ann Hoberman:** 'Tiger' and 'Giraffes' from *The Llama Who Had No Pajama, 100 Favorite Poems* (Harcourt Brace, 1998), copyright © 1959 and renewed 1987 by Mary Ann Hoberman repr. by permission of the publisher and Gina Maccoby Literary Agency. **Julie Holder:** 'The Corn Scratch Kwa Kwa Hen and the Fox' from *Fox Poems* compiled by John Foster (OUP, 1990), repr. by permission of the author. **Martin Honeysett:** 'The Centipedes in the Garden' from *Animal Nonsense* (Methuen Children's Books Limited, an imprint of Egmont Children's Books Ltd, 1984), repr. by permission of the publisher. **Jessie Hope:** 'Our Visit to the Zoo' from *Me Me Me* ed. Dorothy Butler. **Ted Hughes:** 'My Other Folks' from *Meet My Granny* (Faber & Faber, 1961), repr. by permission of the publisher. **Dick King-Smith:** 'The Mole' from *Animal Poems* ed. Meg Rutherford (Simon & Schuster). **Rudyard Kipling:** 'Commissariat Camels' from *The Definitive Edition* (Macmillan, 1940), repr. by permission of A.P. Watt Ltd on behalf of The National Trust for Places of Historical Interest or Natural Beauty. **James Kirkup:** 'Polar Bear' from *Look at It This Way* (Rockingham Press, 1994), repr. by permission of the author. **Patricia Leighton:** 'A New-Born Foal', copyright © Patricia Leighton 2001, first pub. in this collection by permission of the author. **Patrick J. Lewis:** 'Blue Herons', copyright © Patrick J. Lewis 2001, first pub. in this collection by permission of the author. **Elizabeth Madox Roberts:** 'The Woodpecker' from *Under the Tree* copyright 1922 by B. W. Huebsch, Inc., renewed 1950 by Ivor S. Roberts. Copyright 1930 by Viking Penguin, renewed © 1958 by Ivor S. Roberts & Viking Penguin, repr. by permission of Viking Penguin, an imprint of Penguin Putnam Books for Young Readers, a division of Penguin Putnam Inc. **Spike Milligan:** 'A Baby Sardine' from *A Book of Milliganimals* (Penguin, 1971) and 'Tell Me, Little Woodworm' from *Silly Verse for Kids* (Puffin, 1968), both repr. by permission of Spike Milligan Productions Ltd. **Tony Mitton:** 'A Dream of Elephants', copyright © Tony Mitton 1994 first pub. in *A Trunkful of Elephants* ed. Judith Nicholls (Methuen, 1994); 'Meeting the Snake', copyright © Tony Mitton 1996, from *Reptile Poems* ed. John Foster (OUP, 1996), both repr. by permission of the author. 'Robin', copyright © Tony Mitton 2001, first pub. in this collection by permission of the author. **John Mole:** 'The Animal Alphabet', copyright © John Mole 2001, first pub. in this collection by permission of the author. **Pat Moon:** 'Noah's Ark' from *Earthlines* (Pimlico, 1991), copyright © Pat Moon 1991, repr. by permission of the author. **Blake Morrison:** 'Sea Horses' from *Casting a Spell* compiled by Angela Huth (Orchard Books). **Ogden Nash:** 'The Duck' from *Verses From 1929 On* (Dent, 1961). **Judith Nicholls:** 'Tortoise and Hare Poem' from *Midnight Forest* (Faber & Faber, 1987), copyright © Judith Nicholls 1987 and 'Wolf' from *Dragonsfire*, (Faber & Faber, 1990), copyright © Judith Nicholls 1990, both repr. by permission of the author. 'Dolphin Dance', copyright © Judith Nicholls 2001, first pub. in this collection by permission of the author. **Grace Nichols:** 'I'm a Parrot' from *Come into my Tropical Garden* (A & C Black Publishers Ltd, 1988), copyright © Grace Nichols 1988, repr. by permission of Curtis Brown Ltd, London, on behalf of Grace Nichols. **Jack Ousbey:** 'Song of the Ark', copyright © Jack Ousbey 2001, first pub. in this collection by permission of the author. **Jack Prelutsky:** 'The Walrus' from *Zoo Doings* (Greenwillow Books, 1983), copyright © Jack Prelutsky 1983, and 'Late One Night in Kalamazoo' from *Ride a Purple Pelican* (Greenwillow Books, 1986), copyright © Jack Prelutsky 1986, both repr. by permission of HarperCollins Publishers. **James Reeves:** 'Rabbit and Lark' from *Complete Poems for Children* (Heinemann, 1994), copyright © James Reeves, repr. by permission of the James Reeves Estate. **Cynthia Rider:** 'The Peacock', copyright © Cynthia Rider 2001, first pub. in this collection by permission of the author. **Monica Shannon:** 'Only My Opinion' from *Goose Grass*, copyright © 1930 by Doubleday, a division of Bantam Doubleday, Dell Publishing Group Inc., repr. by permission of Doubleday, a division of Random House Inc. **William Jay Smith:** 'Seal' from *Laughing Time: Collected Nonsense* by William Jay Smith, (Farrar, Straus and Giroux, 1990), copyright © William Jay Smith 1990, repr. by permission of the publisher. **Arnold Spilka:** 'Hippopotamuses' from *A Lion I Can't Do Without* (Walck, 1964). **Kaye Starbird:** 'Sparrow' from *Eric Carle's Animal Animal* (Hodder & Stoughton). **Dylan Thomas:** 'Song of Mischievous Dog' from *The Poems of Dylan Thomas* (J. M. Dent), copyright © 1957 by The Trustees for the Copyrights of Dylan Thomas, repr. by permission of David Higham Associates and New Directions Publishing Corp. **Judith Thurman:** 'Mare' from *Flashlight and Other Poems* (Kestrel, 1976), copyright © Judith Thurman 1976, repr. by permission of Marian Reiner Literary Agent on behalf of the author. **John Walsh:** 'Goldfish' from *The Beaver Book of Animal Verse* compiled by Raymond Wilson (Macmillan). **Celia Warren:** 'Penguins on Ice', copyright © Celia Warren 2000, from *Wacky Wild Animals* ed. Brian Moses (Macmillan, 2000), repr. by permission of the author. **Raymond Wilson:** 'Spring' from *Time's Delight* (Hamlyn, 1977), copyright © Raymond Wilson 1977, repr. by permission of G. M. Wilson. **Margaret Wise Brown:** 'The Fish with the Deep Sea Smile' from *Nibble Nibble*, (HarperCollins Inc.), copyright © William R. Scott Inc. 1959, ren. Roberta Brown Rauch 1987, repr. by permission of the publisher. **Kathryn Worth:** 'Circus Elephant' from *A Child's Treasury of Verse* ed. E. Doan (Hodder & Stoughton). **Valerie Worth:** 'Sea Lions' from *All the Small Poems and Fourteen More* (Farrar, Straus & Giroux, 1987), copyright © Valerie Worth 1994, repr. by permission of the publisher. **Kit Wright:** 'Our Hamster's Life' from *Rabbiting On* (Fontana, 1978), repr. by permission of the author. **W. B. Yeats:** 'To a Squirrel at Kyle-na-no' from *Complete Poems* (Macmillan), repr. by permission of W. B. Yeats Ltd on behalf of Michael B. Yeats. **Jane Yolen:** 'Grandpa Bear's Lullaby', first published in *Dragon Night and other Lullabies* (Methuen, 1980), copyright © Jane Yolen 1980, repr. by permission of Curtis Brown, Ltd. **Charlotte Zolotow:** 'Little Bird' from *River Winding* (Abelard-Schuman).

Although we have tried to trace and contact copyright holders before publication, in some cases this has not been possible. If contacted we will be pleased to rectify any errors or omissions at the earliest opportunity.

Song of the Ark

Elephant lives where the grass is high,
Snake where the sun is warm,
Owl has a perch in a large, old tree,
And cow lives on the farm;
Spider spins a silken web,
Mouse makes a nest of straw,
Rabbit's home is a hole in the ground
Dog's in a bed by the door:

Chorus:
   When thunder growls and lightning forks,
   When clouds hang low and dark,
   When the wind is high and the rain beats down
   They come to the big wooden Ark.
   Ark warm—Ark dry,
   Ark so safe and sound,
   Ark is the home where the animals come
   When the waters cover the ground.

Camel lives in a world of sand,
Snail near a garden shed,
Toad in the mud just down by the pool
And cat in a basket bed;
Hippo wallows in a muddy lake,
Butterfly rests on a flower,
Panda's place is a bamboo grove
And bat's a belfry tower.

Chorus:
   When thunder growls and lightning forks,
   When clouds hang low and dark,
   When the wind is high and the rain beats down
   They come to the big wooden Ark.
   Ark warm—Ark dry,
   Ark so safe and sound,
   Ark is the home where the animals come
   When the waters cover the ground.

Jack Ousbey

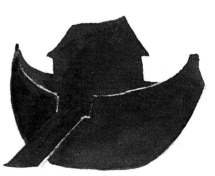